THE WATERTANK REVISITED

DELORES GAUNTLETT

THE WATERTANK REVISITED

PEEPAL TREE

First published in Great Britain in 2005
Peepal Tree Press Ltd
17 King's Avenue
Leeds LS6 1QS
UK

ISBN 1 84523 009 4

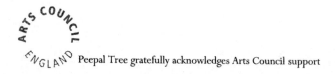 Peepal Tree gratefully acknowledges Arts Council support

CONTENTS

THE WATERTANK REVISITED

Without the weight of what then seemed important,
I returned to the house under the hill
with its old unfinished watertank, teemed now

with shrubs. From its grave, the ants haul their loot.
Bees, wasps and butterflies are inquiring, romancing.

Its bank slippery as papa's dream,
and scattered with tins whose razor tongues
mimic the sun.

It was my father's job to lift the line in the wind
like a billowing sail, before the clothes swiped the dirt,
to split the wood and start the new foundation.

The watertank: half
-sunk in the soil like a stubborn stare,
is the reason I expected more than his best,
gone to weed, too, now; gathering moss.

I ask myself: what does it matter
that piped water was forestalled?
Besides, what's the past but a rainless day

with dry bush rustling the hill,
and a no-longer-flawed perfection
awaiting another dream to beam from a window,

my father's, mine,
and flow like rain to a tar-glazed water drum planked on flat stones,
guttering in song from a roof,

overflowing to a river no one owns?

THE RAINY DAY

Dawn at the kitchen window and rain
pelting the zinc roof in the pallid light,
loud and impatient, choking gutters and
rushing to the water drum planked on stones,
its overflow washing the gravel downhill
flushing past under the coop where the hens rustle,
nesting down in a bed of banana leaves.

The wind quickens through the countryside,
the yellow rose bush thrashes, the coconut leaves
crash about like a wild thing trapped in a net,
with each gust
the overripe Seville oranges lose their grip and fall.
In the lightning's livid silence
the rain overruns all other sounds
except the heavy rolling of the thunderstruck hillside.
I crouch behind the sill. No pigeons
woo the morning with their little liquid songs.

This is not a morning for school,
for the trek down the hillside where the billy goats bleat
their welcome, munching from tuft to tuft,
for the 90-minute walk, going and coming
with the road to ourselves, and loud laughter.
By the stone wall where lizards scoot
and galliwasps flick out their silent tongues
in the field, a line of cows, heads down
in the drenched pangola grass, flick their tails,
and a black-bellied heifer with a wobbly calf
bellows suddenly against the rain and wind,
as though it might wake the cow gods from their deep sleep
to come and save the herd from misery.

The rain subsides;
the second hand of the kitchen clock ticks
in time with the last drops dripping from the roof.
A laying hen, filling its craw, cackles.

My father returns from the garden,
having quieted the pigs' squealing obscenities.
He stomps the mud from his wet black water-boots
into the door mat, the ripples of plaited straw.

A QUESTION OF LOVE

Back when I used to play doctor: I am
passing the house with its blinds fully pulled;
the boarded-up window facing the road
nails out the past from what they say love did
to the girl at a city school. Three years
she's been in that room with her diary of hurt.
What stalks her mind robs her of speech.
Like a slate wiped clean, she returns to the bed
that is her fort against the overhang
of whatever fills her mind with its long night.
To hush the shame, no one's invited there.
That house: above eye level from the road,
with whitewashed stones up to the verandah steps
forming two lines from the gate! A hard wind flaps
a nearby breadfruit tree as I pass,
marvelling at what the adults deem
might be fruit for a juicy conversation,
blind to the secret in the children's game
of *Thread yuh needle, thread, oh, long, long thread,*
while she, stuck in a world she cannot
leave behind her, lurks in a room
whose curtain never moves in the wind.

A SENSE OF TIME

I drive past my father's grave
and past the place where I began.
That swing-bridge to my childhood games
is now a town to which I seldom return.
There the headstones wear familiar names,
and there I turned the page
at five to my first big word,
repeating it until it blurred.

The church grew smaller in the rear
-view mirror; my face awash in the wind,
I approached the curves I knew by heart,
then drove the silent miles to Flat Bridge.
The sun going down behind the hill
hauled its net of shadow as it fell.

MY MOTHER'S SILENCE,
MY FATHER'S STARE

What did I know at nine about the human heart
to know what I was learning? That my mother's strength
lay in her knowing what should be passed over,
that her silence would survive my father's stare,
stalling the anger of the day from flaring,
knowing just what to do with his raised brow.
She was the house with the slant roof under the hill,
and he, the unbent pimento tree
towering over her. Its softer roots no one got to know.

Outside, and in the past, where dreams were not achievable,
in black water-boots and garden clothes, he'd bolt
out through the back door at nights to God knows what,
while we children, ignorant of the word 'shellshocked',
braced in the dark, slept off the hours of uncertainty.
Once mama explained the role the full moon played,
that it swung open a door on his World War days.

On Sundays, after the home-parched hot-coffee smell
of good intentions, he wore a different face
to church, taking it off again when he returned.
His best was then obscured by the fear
I wanted to grow up away from and fall in love.
He held the key that kept us from going astray,
she, the lamp left on in the doorway.

AT 50

(ten years later)

You returned to the house and found your father dead.
You cannot face his photograph,
you still turn your head away, tight-lipped,
from the dread recollection
of what hit you so hard you forgot
what day it was:

Something to be found only in a memory
now silenced at the edge of a world
where something other than grief is alive;
something with an undecipherable name
held in place by a night that refuses to pass over –
the only subject on which you cannot lie –
impinging on a nerve
you've learned to ignore:
something I cannot measure.

BACKWARDS UP A SLIPPERY SLOPE

Through the late afternoon, by a stirring sea,
the sunset an hour off, I'm in a trance
watching the riled waves changing shape.
Something takes me back to my parents' house
in broad daylight, and I think of my brother,
remembering the day he told his first lie,
hardly out of the crib, barefaced and brawny:
a lie which, compared to our lies,
was quite out of line, obdurate,
and poised to last beyond a passing phase.

We didn't know then the practice would grow up
to become the dark of a world in which
he foraged in expensive thoughts,
walking backwards up a slippery slope
from one fiction to the next.
Wherever I look, I find, in place of light,
this or that event frozen in a limbo,
waiting for him to get the answers right.

Armed with the history of his Nemesis,
returning to where it began, backdates us 40 years
to his tea cooling in an enamel mug;
despite what the belt burned into him
he arrives at the same place, year after year.
Not knowing where he will be heading next,
I dig my toes into the shifting sand
and watch the heaving sea repeatedly hurl
itself at a rock which doesn't budge.

ON GROWING TIRED OF HER COMPLAINTS

One pound of fretting can't repay one ounce of debt.
(Jamaican Proverb)

As far away as you are now from childhood
is the gap between ideas and reality,
the air tensed with what you took pleasure in,
doodling in complaints, not knowing what to do –
not knowing what accidental turn you took,
that blew everything entirely out of whack
though the worst of the rain has come and gone.
Surrounded by whatever else you happened on,
numbed by repetition, eyes clenched,
you cannot catch the rhythm of the wind,
indecipherable; you move from room to room.

I knew you when a day made a difference,
when you'd look out of the window and gaze
at anything: a bee, the dew drop from a leaf
in the spot by the still pond under the trees.
Now you linger by the bridge where what's unlived
is not available, where even a mild occurrence
shapes a stronghold of might-have-been, of this and that;
and nothing I say today
will be any more convincing than the last.
Meantime the rest of the world unfurls, shading
the retreating back of history, and what happens, happens.

VISITING HER DEAD HUSBAND'S SISTER

Something has locked their tongues for thirty years —
something extreme. Yet now, with nothing said
of the long years of bitching, they greet with a hug
as if to bridge the past, and define
a lifetime of each one's hoarding of her rights
upon the earth. The hug stops short of their shoulders touching.
Each, turning gray, has her separate ailments,
but now the past pours out like falling rain
with much to be talked about in the narrow room
whose window opens on the abrupt back yard
that stops at a steep climb up from the marl hill
where, a bleat away, goats are picking
through shade and the dry leaves drift unswept.

I sit in silence and watch them break
their silence as time unfolds.
They tiptoe in words around the hard times,
but success is harder to discuss.
The story rests between them like a book
left open between one chapter and the next,
its left-hand pages, already broken in,
telling that there's nothing left to dwell upon.

AFTER THE ARGUMENT

Strange that you have not learned from it:
the reason you backed away for good one day

when, having your own way, and without the least bit
of hesitation, with no impulse to obey,

you washed your hands of what our father said.
I remember that October day. You left the gate ajar,

storming past the stubborn rose bed
which parted a circle in the corner of the yard,

forgetting out of habit to stop and latch
its wood pin, leaving without a word. I watched

the silence grow. The variegated Joseph coat

wakes the soul of that memory, and today
I come to tell you that I understand,

trying to write that no matter how much we weigh
the past, there are things which do not meet the eye, and

explain how I see a new generation at the door
where history repeats; to write that it takes

a long time sometimes to bridge the gap before
we arrive at the root of our own mistakes;

that I remember the day we drove in silence
through slanting rain, wracked as in a dream,

imagining his final words and picking sense
from his letter to the grandchild he'd never seen.

SILENCE

The night our marriage failed a full moon
drifted its bald silence above the sill,

halting a cut of moonlight in the empty room.
The lamp turned off, the past collated, and as still

as a glass shattering to silence, the time was spent,
the wedding photographs nowhere in sight.

I lost your face to the shadow of a distant
memory on the day your beard grew overnight,

to the night your eyes took on a stranger's look
when even the threat of burglary did not

inject new meaning into our vow. Like a closed book
whose words no longer reassured, time locked

away the things we left unsaid, politely
far from interpretation. The rest unveiled

itself as the morning arrived, quietly.
The year I left was not the year it failed.

Something of time sank with every birthday missed
and/or ignored, with every spite; with me being

caught in a silence that no longer reminisced,
and you seemingly untouched by everything.

THE FEVER WITH WHICH SHE DANCED

Readying herself for what's to come, she turns
to another life, to which she's come to let go,
clap hands and dance, and dream of the place
where a bed overlooks the healing waters' flow,
and a soul wings it over the fields
to whatever lulls her from past conditions,
removing the mask to make peace with grief,
unblinkingly suspending the world elsewhere.

She takes sorrow to where all sense breaks loose
as though possessed, thrown into ecstasy,
singing up the nothingness, free from excuse
in a roomfull of women chanting unknown tongues
while the sole man waves his Bible like a flag of truce,
tip-toeing, prompting the chant, as if to see
into the reaches of their silences
calling forth hallelujahs without apologies.

She takes her respite up St. Peter's Hill
towards the precious fountain, where morning kneels
to admit those things she cannot dismiss,
bearing the moment to a basic blank,
lingering in the shadow of her own free will
where every limb lets go – miming words,
entranced, erasing the onlooker: such was
the fever with which she danced.

LOVE CHANGES EVERYTHING

At the window where our two reflections
meet, pulled as to a magnet to the rhythm
of Zamfir's panflute whistling its seduction
Love, love changes everything...
Sometimes the body needs to set itself on fire,
to consume the dry leaves and twigs as if swept
by a magic wind to a new view of desire,
barefoot, heart racing from the outset,
flayed like an upheld palm in the rain.
Then work defers to moments that assume
good reason to be here and love, not live in vain,
gauging time like an echo in a vacant room.
We, once strangers on the eve of first sight,
blush through blue August, whispering goodnight.

LIKE ANY OTHER BRIDE

Like any other bride, she held the flame
of contemplated bliss, swayed from the edge
of spinsterhood to sharing a common name,
walking the aisle to what the vows alleged.
Doubting the wisdom of some early signs
wavering between a maze of kids and the man
with whom the final word reclined,
she carried the hurt discreetly as it began.
Walking on shells in an attempt to keep
the half-hid secrets while the heart subsided
against a wall with things to escape in sleep,
alluding to a dream which coincided
with the soul seeking its own salvation,
she turned a blind eye to the blazing sun.

MY FIRST KISS

On the night of my first kiss, unsteadied by bliss,
a brisk wind mused in the navel-orange leaves
as despite all warnings, my curiosity whisked
me to the window where the flame of youth breathed
on certain things apt to be kept low-keyed
when dormant feelings rise from secret floors,
increasingly curious, yet not allowed to read
the amazing book stashed behind closed doors.
I was moved to ecstasy; I felt I had sinned;
I swore that my skirts were tightening,
and, like a fool, I starved myself
to abort what I'd been imagining.
Sick with the fear of being expelled from school,
I jumped from a swing to put everything right,
to halt that conception from coming to light.

ANOTHER MYSTERY OF LOVE

He loved her, but he used his love like a rope:
frayed from their tug-of-war of the heart,
stretched taut across his frightening temper
till he fell flat on his back to win.
Meanwhile she slipped away with something heartrending
caught in her eye,
diverting her attention by making bread,
kneading until the sun burned out,
slapping the dough with the heel of her hand
to revenge herself
against the familiar words which quailed her
into thinking everything she did was wrong.
Then he, looking as though it had never happened,
and she, never looking at another man,
stared out of the window, wondering at the bird
clinging to a swaying stalk in silence,
waiting
like a patient thought.

LOVE LETTERS

At first it was your slick quips
that quickened me to sit down and take notice –
when to my one-sentence reply you said
I reminded you of Lord Wavell,
the British general in World War II
who, the more adulation he received,
the more taciturn he became,
that brevity, brevity was his forte,
that his strength lay in silence.

That was the hook that lifted my attention,
and when it seemed you guessed what I was wearing
the first intensity warmed the air to now.
You wound me a path along windswept beaches
to a place unmarked on any map
where we resumed our secret walk with words
guardedly wrapped around ourselves,
though between each line the meaning was implied.

And when I wrote to you my reason
why I couldn't meet you face to face, I lied.
I wanted instead to lean into your hands
away from the tangibles of daily life,
wearing the countenance that each word bears
where nothing is well founded; yet
when you invited me to sit down, and I did,
I understood *more* and *less* at the same time.

THE MORNING AFTER

Behind the strangeness in your eyes
on that kissless morning after the night before
there's nothing bright for gathering.
The silence squatting upon the room
where the waltz began to the unchained
melody and the hungry touch
now owns the things we used to say.
I know there's someone else out there,
some life you have to touch
with the lull of your cologne and the song
I thought my own;
I know there are other things knocking around
in your heart from which memory refuses to budge.

It's over, love. In the clanging of plates
as if the whole world should hear
and doing a day's housework in an hour,
I know the old words are as useless as my hands
to ignite the hunger that was once there
or rip the cloud asunder.
Drifting between two worlds
of being in love, being out of love,
with sad music on my mind
and the still half-wished-for things withdrawing,
now more than a touch away,
I tell myself it's better this way.

LUST

If only she could touch him,
hear his knock on her door,
feel her pulse approaching!
She longs to draw the shades,
lock hands as tight as prose,
give voice to that voice otherwise unused.

She smiles a little to herself
without musing, Whom will he marry?
She thinks: If this is one of seven
downfalls, it's the border of in-between,

where to get in touch and where to touch
are as good as breathing,
and closer than word of mouth.

She longs to be a map
without a sign for Caution,
to feel his fingernails trailing
its contours, north to south.

VALENTINE'S DAY

If we are facing in the right direction,
all we have to do is keep on walking.
(Ancient Buddhist Proverb)

It is a day we may acknowledge or ignore —
a day when love goes on parade
piping through the labyrinth of the world,
when expectation's on edge;
a day when a thick fog fringes offshore,
keeping the sun at bay, like a note that never comes,
while a whispering breeze riffles the leaves
with a free hand, bringing the welcome thought
that if we are facing in the right direction
all we have to do is keep on walking.
It's a day when love swings both high and low,
joy and discontent sharing the same room
while Valentine's Day feeds on its flame.
Around it I skirt to find a starting line
to this verse, watching the parade go by.

LOVE REKINDLED

Ol' firestick easy fi ketch.
Jamaican Proverb

Now that they have come to look at love
with the hindsight of how well the good old days
flash back, time melts the silence away,
and the years between them disappear.
They are drawn to the half-burnt firewood
left in a field where the past now rests its case,
holding something faintly familiar,
blowing in a wind from out of nowhere,
finding the spark that crackles the wood
towards which they step, to be in touch again!

Now that they have come to look at love
with a familiar eye, the Muse of bliss
rests near the embers of their souls.
He is the stillness of that spring,
the heart of what was never quite done,
that which fills a hollow house;
while she with confidence moves on
from the consolidation of the years
towards whatever the future brings.

READING BETWEEN THE LINES

Shifting from the edge of the day's uncertainties
to the hazy comfort of our long-distance love,
finding it easy to wonder what you're doing,
then wonder why I'm wondering
about someone I'll never meet face-to-face one day,
in the still air, I open your card to find
a brown bull sporting a red rose between its teeth.

I settle in, roaming the hidden reaches
of its meaning, shifting from one point of view
to the next, to the code-breaking edge of thought,
from the missing thorns to the colour of the rose,
and I tell myself that it must mean something else –
something beyond your accompanying words,
something as deep and open as the seas between us.

With only a photo of you in mind
I follow my thoughts, as with a psychic force,
to the mantelpiece on which we pose
in turtleneck pullovers: a safe place for the heart
in the midnight rhetoric of what might be
if you were here instead of over there.
You, in the land of The Rising Sun, and I
in the quiet syntax of the afternoon
pressing back against a chair with what it brings,
drifting, without pinpointing what unfolds,
in a thought in which I could easily grow old.

THE DANCE

No need to guess where he's at today:

this is the hour to dance the time away,
to steal each other's heart with eyes closed,
touch hands and listen without words,

with the song a breath away, composed
between two sets of feet taking the same
steps twice:

the shore of love,
the world at bay,
the night assured
of being remembered by

Once, twice, three times a lady

while you and I swing to a glance,
a clear sign, and the search for dancing-room
for this cadence.

WRITING A POEM IN METER

Takes rain, the racket
in a madman's head
and strains
it into sonata.
(Wayne Brown: 'Critic')

Nothing on the page made sense.
I was on the brink of giving up
fretting in pentameter,
feeling like a fish pulled from the sea
into the fierce sunlight,
when your no-fooling-around approach
and a direct heart sent me to work.
That each line should slip under the skin,
as in the blood, fleshed out from the nuance
of sound on sound, as in the beat of a heart!
I pushed off into the swell,
swimming across the bay of iambics:
three, four, five beats underwater,
pulling, pulling against the tension,
taking a turn on my back,
watching the water scatter from my hands,
splash, splash, each slow spondee
stretching my thought beyond recollection.

Call it the music in the traffic-hiss,
entertaining an early morning thought,
or the climb uphill to the first clearing
to move around in when a foot doesn't fit.
To one who asks
'What's the good of all that?'
I can only speak for me,
that it discovers what I have to say,
takes my hand and leads me down a lane
from which I can take my time returning.

BODY AND SOUL

Soul says it's the one who does the dreaming.
It complains that Body drives it nuts

standing before the open refrigerator
an hour past midnight

and grumbles about having to carry Body everywhere
as though it were some unspeakable habit.

Body asks with a smirk who hurts more,
and who taught whom to swim.

Soul tells Body it watches the whole shebang
and is strong enough to be silent,

that it softens the sharp edges
of isolation and can leave whenever it wants,

that it has snuck out many a night
down the slant of the roof

and returned through the locked door before sunrise
like a shadow pouring into water,

singing old hymns from the depth of its lungs
as if each word were new,

while Body stood idly by,
thinking of faces they have both known.

Body says that without it Soul would be a flame
guttering in the wind without a candlestick;

that it's the window through which Soul breathes
and the heartbeat that owns the house.

Soul says nothing. It gives Body a look that says:

I'm what silence holds in store for you.

THE BIRD

On a leafless bough up there
a bird shook free from the dew,
then eagerly combed the air
for something else to do.

Listening to what's being said
in the woods, it catches its meal
and swallows. What it hears
the breeze conspires to conceal:

That undreamt phase of Death
beyond any change of mind,
as blameless as the shadow
that leaves the mourner behind.

Over the careworn world
it flies on mirroring wings
up into the white shine of the sky
(slipping my grasp) and sings.

THAT SUNDAY MORNING

She was not begging for forgiveness when she knelt
facing the wall, her head flung back
as if preparing to hold a flashlight to the eyes of Jesus.
Full of argument, raw with energy,
something shouting in her breast flashed clear again
to the August afternoon when the death winds came
to the broken sidewalk that narrows to a lane,
when, after the bullet wrapped itself in silence,
it took the colour from the photo in her purse.

She looked in vain for answers
to what nags her sleep, night after night,
remembering the hour when the sun went down burning
over the yard of scratching chickens, digging
for the words that would tell her all would be well
while the clock ticked to the wrong time.
Talking to Him as if to a next door neighbour
she stood, knowing her anger was not a bluff,
and, with the world still coming to an end,
danced her way up to a victory hallelujah! –
a pitch this poem cannot put into 20 lines.

INTRODUCTION TO POETRY

(For Mervyn Morris)

'I wish you'd write some foolishness sometimes,'
you said in that workshop off South Camp Road,
and it took some years to uncover what you meant:
To bring out what I'd seen, or wished I'd seen,
in a simple line
and state outright that this is it;
to find my way out of the cul-de-sac,
when trying too hard, wide of the mark,
the words coming but not the sense;
to balance each line and not feel the weight;
to watch day break across a familiar land,
freeing the verse as on a passing wind;
to walk all night under a changing moon.
To convert the outrage into song, the poem coming,
not as from the space between
a sleepwalker's outstretched arms,
but as in a hand held still against rushing water,
then lifted clear, the drops from the dripping
fingertips settling in the poem's room.

THE RISING WATER

In my recurring dream I'm always lost,
always climbing up a crooked familiar path,
running away from threatening waters
clear as glass and just flat –
water rising in a tranquil, sunless light,
not hissing nor spraying nor churning out groans,
no fish swirling around each other,
no shadows changing in the wind –
not water to toss a pebble in and watch the ripples spread –
just still water, rising.

The more I climb, the more the water rises,
the mountain seeming to expand
with every step as I pick my way uphill
through dense ferns, with not a bird in sight,
hauling my fear up through brambles,
through the high grass wet with dew,
crossing an unknown river turning in its bed,
passing some strangers along the way,
while the still water rises, drowning everywhere I've been.

Then, no sooner safe, far enough
from the shoreless water, I turn to look down
and, just as suddenly, the water vanishes.
But now, facing the long descent,
I find the old path existed in my mind only,
and feel like one who wakes in a strange place.
The track now divides into a labyrinth,
leading nowhere, ending where it began,
and the harder I try to find my way
the more I am trapped in that no-man's-land,
between an inner and outer world,
gone from my time into another,
too confused even to rest beneath a tree.

And I think perhaps death will be like this:
finding myself in between worlds
I cannot enter, not knowing whether to retreat
or continue into that separate night,
barefoot, watching birds breaking awake.

THIS MORNING

Nothing else relates to today.
Outside the beach house the morning unwinds
the sea breeze. I rise and switch off the news –
news that causes the jaw to drop –
then go and sit in the hillside's shade
overlooking the sea
at a careful distance from the edge.
The sun bulbs over the mountain.
Between waves engendered by a departing ship
and coming ashore now, roar after roar,
a blue silence each time returns.

Among wild orchids and brambles,
thick leaves and the dew they collected,
I dream on this limestone hillside.
A bird chirps in branches so low they sweep the ground,
and my soul leans out as from an open window
into that world where time takes you in
to itself; where like a kite
memory frolics in the air
as if there were no strings, and I see

a lover's smile, and recall his corny pitch
that nonetheless followed me home
dancing with the shadows of a windy tree,
like a beating heart.

The wind rises, and a grassquit's song
rises from the lignumvitae, an antenna for its young.
Too light for rain, a thin cloud drifts
its unshed tears across my face. Now the sun lifts
up into the sky, spreading its flame,
undressing the mountain by slow degrees,
lifting its filmy gown to disclose
feet firmly on the ground.

THE LIGHTHOUSE

Darkness reigns at the foot of the lighthouse.
(Japanese Proverb)

Some distance off from where the water comes
and goes, rubbing out footprints in the sand,
the lighthouse lifts its lamp as the day succumbs
to an after-twilight weaving deep inland,
a dark more certain than tomorrow's weather,
a dark that keeps us guessing as in a blindfold
outside its corridor while it comes together
in a dead silence upon which there's no foothold.
Yet the light ignites that which we seek,
that which the soul strives to discover
as when you stroke the rose you cannot keep,
bidding the seaman to the shore of his lover,
glowing unquenched to the sighs of deep relief
while the riled sea rocks back upon itself.

AT GUNPOINT

(for my brother, Junior)

The world contracts
around one voice, 'Pussy, nuh move yuh nuh,'
and the poke of cold metal in his side
driving him into the bushes of disbelief.
Face down in dirt, under a quiet sky,
next to a blooming macka, begging for his life,
his infant son flashes before him at the same time
as his Saviour upon the Cross,

and he finds a loophole and runs for his life
over the broken barbed wire fence and into the street;
his livelihood disappears down the road
dragging the keys to his spirit;
the pocket to his heart has been emptied.

He is not yet glad to be alive.
The day hardens to the reality of walking home
and a face he'll never forgive.

That night, under the balm of olive oil and a mother's thumb,
a streetlamp glows on a bed
where hurt turns again to dread
and he writhes, writhes,
and survives.

SHADOW

The sun pulling the shadow toward the hill,
seeming to scan the page of a book left carelessly open,
is proof some things move ahead of understanding.
You are the path between two houses,
the door drawn at the usual time each evening
sheltering the grass; weightlessly shifting your shape,
distracting the gaze of the blazing sun.
You are the truth without a face under which to lie,
and, without doubt, a tenacious witness,
not responsible for what you know.
You go from how things seem to what they are,
stick to me like a trail of melted candle
that never anchors my steps. Incorrigibly you,
you are the drifter of the dance,
and we, motive and act, sanctioned in one bed.
When I touch you, nothing clasps my hand.

THE BROKEN LOOKING-GLASS

Found by the sun

the chip of mirror blazes
from the hillside like the truth it's known to tell,

morse-coding beyond breaking point
to a world where hurt comes home to everyone,

where every point of view sparks something else
and a moment mirrors everything.
Where memory wakes up remembering to forget

while the sun plays at seeing its own face
in the first glint of morning, hunting the hill.

The chip of mirror blazes
from the hill with the truth it knows too well.

SUNRISE OVER BLUE MOUNTAIN

Guilt stops at the doorway to that room
in the lower hill which I call my fort
against the things I cannot change,
where I stop looking over my shoulder,
having given all I have to give:
that room dusted with memories
where uncertainty hides the key to knowing
what causes a love to be quelled.

I think of the fogged-in trail
on that Sunday morning of the hike
from Portland Gap, pushing up to the rocks
through the woodland bushes,
breaking the brambles like fingernails,
wearing out a new divorce...

The others pick up the pace,
flashlights and voices prove the way ahead
sorting through the early morning dark,
timing the climb to the rising sun,
I chant: *I am climbing Jacob's Ladder...*

I cross the shallow stream heading down,
stepping on stones in the blind path
with crickets sawing the fog
and the wind cold; combing the ground for frost
I look up to a sky
towards which I cannot hurry,
I rest at the foot of an unknown tree. Each mile
bringing into focus my fear of being lost.
'I am climbing Jacob's Ladder...'

At the top, the spirit leaps
as if to see how well we grow wings at any age.
A breathless thought, easier than understanding,
charms my attention to the rising sun
bursting beyond the rocks overlooking Cuba.

THE RECKONING

A nuh di same day leaf drop in a water it rotten.
(Jamaican Proverb)

Years later, he walks beside the shadow
of the past, to the beat of the grim consequences
he brought upon himself in surprising ways.
In middle-age he might have been content,
had he foreseen that as time went by
his antics would lead to where love pulled away
to be as far from him as possible
when his expression betrayed no signs of change.
Blinded to the cause of his predicament,
he walks, with nothing open for discussion,
not knowing he's been struck by his own hand.

IN LIMBO

Yuh cyan sow corn and expec' fi reap peas.
(Jamaican Proverb)

Unable in the end to separate what's done from what
should have been done, the truth
undid what you so earnestly embodied.

There's nothing for it:
your life requires a harder pardon.
Cry all you want,

but for a miracle: your promises have gone
like smoke
on a stray breeze up into a cloud,

gray from overuse,

a cloud from which the night fills in
the disquiet of the past,
and what was hidden is rising

to the surface, like a dank mist after rain.

MIRROR

If there's more to this mirror
that's what I'm looking at;
though, in its otherworldliness,
the obvious is difficult to see.

If there's some secret this mirror knows
that secret begins where it ends:
this wordless watcher whose eye reflects
the dream in which we move and feel no pain.

I watch it watching me, and what comes to mind
is puzzling. I think, *Leave well alone*.
This mirror handles weight as though weight were a cliché.

I'm the one who gives in and looks away.

FOR RALPH THOMPSON

I have in mind the poem I wrote
three years ago, my best till then
(according to someone who knows),

the poem I could not bring myself to look at
after it failed in a competition,
and, though other poems had failed before and after it,
became the one I grew to hate.

Until the year it crossed your path
and came back to me with your pencilled-in
comment which this poem will not name,
but which, like a delayed reaction,

slowly drew the poison that seeped
into me like ink into blotting paper,
and returned the poem like a whispering heart
dangling its locket, restoring what was lost

"close to blue August and the sand-kept shores
of seven seas".

UNDRESSING

Not quite in a hurry, but anxious to shed,
like rain from a leaf the blue skirt
tumbles to a puddle on the floor; the empty blouse,
the bra undone, thrown onto the back of a chair,
still warm, hold the faint smell of body oil.
Like coming out of sleep with a forgotten dream
given back to the night wind whence it came,
the clothing no longer moves when I move.

So, stepping out of a hard day at work,
escaping into nothing, seeking nothing in return,
as a flower is blown when its bloom is done,
I trail along the bank of an afterthought,
my mood swinging into that which water cannot wet,
that which gives the soul its breathing space,
while silence rocks the hour into those
other inchoate and unpredicted things

coming full circle to what tomorrow brings.

FORGETFULNESS

This morning I awoke to the random words
of a full sentence from the freshness of a dream,
lurking in the shadows, stalled in a familiar place.
It slipped before I could put my finger on it
and vanished quicker than a second thought
through the lattice-work of memory,
giving the appearance, if not of disappointment,
of a passing dream given back to the gods,
or a moment with no before and after,
a noun freed from designation.
I closed my eyes, thinking if I did not move
something might retrieve it and row it back
towards even a vague impression of it,
on the verge of discovery, to be stumbled on,
recovering it from where it fell tight-lipped.   .
With no choice but to leave it along the way,
accepting it was not something to hound down,
I told myself it was already said and done
and came merely to raise an alarm, perhaps,
to something else in the hollows of my mind.

FIREFLY

In the last stanza of the evening sun
two lovers sip red wine on a bench faked
to look like wood, rooted under a banyan tree
centuries wide, shading the secrets of the lawn
from all that has to come to pass
on this Firefly Hill, 1200 feet up from the sea,
with a riffling breeze caught in its leaves.

From this spot of indecipherable charm,
the blue sea turns gray, as though acknowledging the dusk,
while its eternal velvet foil ripples and rocks,
and wave after wave quenches itself
in the endless sand. A mast gestures from afar
at the back of the sky, as if in debate,
moving neither fast nor slow. A gull circles,
with the grace of acceptance, away from the dying sun.

As at the end of some sentence with a thought
left unsaid, a large orange moon rises on cue
from the depth of whatever swallowed everything alive,
bulging with silence, breaking the night's reflection;
out of long habit, the hour darkens in moonlight.
In this slow penumbra, which ages in a jiffy,
on a marble plot on par with the grass,
a child dances in circles on Noel Coward's grave
unaware of what the past has up its sleeve.

GHOST

Somewhere around the corner
of Afterlife – past the memory of light
your soul runs into itself

while you build up to a smoke, in solitude, and
like a spinning gig of cottonball
spiral off some wall of time

leafing through old letters
in a dusty archive.
To appease the disconnection

you're presented with a ritual dance
around the belief of melting candles
intended to free your spirit from any loose end

while it transcends this in-between.
I hear that you visit old enemies
to drop fear into their hearts.

At best, you respect a Holy Book.
At worst, you leave no breath of warning
on the mirror, having come to the brink,

rocking an empty chair,
watching dead uncles playing dominoes:
and you're supposed to rattle teacups – so I hear.

CROAKER

The croaking lizard crawls out
from a place it's not supposed to be,
leaping at a moth, transforming me
into a fluent flow of anger.
This room is not big enough
for both of us. The muse
of the next poem whisked away,
the music of the evening raindrops lost,
I realise there's no one else:
the problem is mine alone.

I will it to make a careless move
and coincide with the slap of the broom
as I brace myself, insecticide at hand,
foraging in the fear I must contain.
It's not like the fear that lurks when I see
the gap between platform and moving train;
this fear's worse. Not daring to take
my eyes away, I time its next move –

but, quicker than quicksilver,
after staring at me as if I,
not it, were the son-of-a-bitch,

it disappears behind the glass-framed picture.

THE PEN

Emerging from the dream with a full sentence
nagging at my mind on the verge of wearing out,
I fumble for the purple pen
between the silence and the words.
The room's pitch black.

In the notebook fumblingly
found next to my pillow
I judge the margin of each line.
The pen pulses; the stream is liquid,
it flows without a hitch:

Words to be examined later
for some undemonstrative metaphor or
iambic spirit liquid enough
to flow into itself, like rain,
or recede into nothing in particular.

The storm settles.
My mind, not yet craving its completion,
pitches past the dream with little memory of it.
The scrawled lines uncoil in the midnight dark.
The pen taps idly on the page in contemplation.

With whatever motive binds the muse,
like a lover holding a letter to the light
I fish for something to modify
the image, and mirror the words –
my pen, not writing; held.

A BOOK OF VERSE, A GLASS OF WINE

'But my joy was too much for display;
it needed the space for silence.'
(Edward Baugh: 'Travelling Man')

When the professor tilted the mike and turned
the page after dinner to his feature address,
to the gathering, anticipating wit, he began:
'Here with a loaf of bread beneath the AC unit,
A book of verse, a glass of wine and Thou
Beside me singing in the Terra Nova tent,
And tent were Paradise enow,'
(With apologies to 'The Rubaiyat of Omar Khayyam').

A singing bird circled inside the tent
in the post-meal December night
and broke out in song in the midst of everything
as if to accompany the glinting words.
The speech was about how not to make a speech;
through it each phrase's after-image
trailed in the mind, to be later held to the light,
stepping back to ensure nothing was missed.
It was a speech in which one registered
the stage on which language was alive and well,
as it was his tone of voice, turned up a notch,
that added the prop which kept the mind aloft
to keep pace with his deep rapport with words,
while the speech did exactly what it said it wouldn't do.

YELLOW POUI

(for Jason)

There's nothing in this frame except the poui
spilling to a pond of fire, at odds with time,
its hour of gold under the blue
on the canvas of the sublime.

You'd have been 26 next month
but for that night your mother won't forget
when you didn't come home, while the uncooked rice
swelled in its water, and the table was never set.

A night stripped of all sense! Now, when I ask
about her soul, she says: 'Lawd! Mi nuh know,
mi nuh know,' as if a roof had caved in
on the task given the alien in her heart.

Like the tree with its bent shadow thrown back
and its losses unredeemed, as is the plight
when Reality shows up on the beaten track
while each bud steps down the ladder with the light

in silence; and yet its melody lingers longer than doubt.
On this April day, each bud propellers down
to the grass, each shading each, each blessing the ground,
not grasping anything, but dwelling in

the importance of today, blazing its all.
In this frame, there's no field beyond the field; no wall.

SOMEWHERE

*'...reaching the other shore of the sea which has
no other shore.'*
(Pablo Neruda: 'The Watersong Ends')

Somewhere beyond the twilight's brilliant showing,
when the good night has taken back the sky,
there's a land safely beyond experience
on the other side of Time: a wordless place
without distances, like a deep memory,
a dark doorway at the corner of the mind
where questions and answers are intertwined
and the silence is transformed
by a bird that wakes and sings, no matter what.
Somewhere the soul stirs in a different armoury,
like a diamond missing from its setting,
stripped of all doubt, flying over the hills,
crossing the rainbow, seamless as music,
while an eternal ladder climbs into a void
between the extremes of this world and the next,
and, from its first rung, time darkens
to clarity –
not like anything in that repeating dream
in which I freefall from a great height,
but as in the realm of an unwritten poem.

GRIEF

Your flare too bright for sight, you're felt,
not seen. On a brisk wind
you arrive, without sufficient reason,
a lost ghost too far astray.
Up from beyond the wide waters, you climb
the roaring waves, pitching your dangerous wings,
cantilevered at the edge where the river runs still
and nothing goes to plan.

Tunneling against the dark
on a path already taken,
not knowing when to say goodbye,
you rivet your unconscious power
to a high so suddenly that wishing
seems to do what prayer has not,

and when you take your final steps inside
the house, shattering my composure,
there's no room to turn around in.
No room to grin and bear it,
when your touch ignites
the soul to go in search of a prop,
to make some use of this,
in a world that will never again be
as it was.

ALONE WITH OTHERS

It happened. *Why not to you instead?* you've asked
of nothing that answers back; no gesture from the hand
of chance to stop the source of that coincidence.
Alone with others, dodging the worn-out question
How are you feeling? barely holding yourself together,
knowing you are not dreaming: There lies the child.
The damp handkerchief like a stone in your fist,
you kneel for the Lord's prayer, losing a line or two,
waiting for some kind muse to resurrect the past,
as when an echo returns from the deeper woods.

You are still here, because on that October day
when the clock stopped like a comma (with nothing else besides),
when its coil unwound, and the world was an open wound,
you faced, as on a fast-moving train
the path on which you were heading, watching the rest rewind.
Here, because you cannot read the future
in the back of a mirror; because the hills won't yield;
because the night is dark, though the moon scythes
shadows into the trackless woods; and we live to learn
that the time we'd like it to be is always overrun
by the time it is.

JASON: 1975 – 1999

It was not your wish
to suspend the mornings of this world,
to disappear in the dead of night
leaving us outside.

There are things we do not know
beyond the shadow of that door
where a whole world is submerged,
but we know that something of you
which death cannot diminish, stays:

Something throttling like a heart,
that resurrects the sun
morning after morning, breaking the dark,
reminding us we're not alone.

I remember the year you turned eight,
with your unruly stub of hair,
and the day you called your mother Judy,
and the day you recovered her pins from the floor
and cushioned them in a row for safekeeping.

I remember the joy in your eyes
when you went down the road with your father,
pointing at this or that, calling his attention
to the latest model of this or that car,
dreaming away your shyness.

Across the picket fence of yesterday,
there's a yard with the dogs you adored,
and the Chinese jimbilin tree
next to the blooming ixora hedge of ginger lily-red.

You cannot be nudged from this sleep;
yet, like the sea, whose each wave
watches the next one coming in
under an orphaned moon still taking time to shine,
is my vigil of memory.

Judy, the summer's gone,
the whistler whistles from an unfamiliar dawn.
One day, while hanging out your socks to dry,
you turned, and the door slammed shut.

Jay-Jay, put your shoes by the door!

TWO WORLDS

Somewhere a child is sifting dust
through his fingers like an hourglass,
each grain following the flow that leads to the past.
Elsewhere a child chases chickens in the yard.
Each is in a playground where
imagination is pitched with activity.
Doing different kinds of the same thing
plumbing the same depth of human possibility.
Somewhere a child picks up a red ball
lying in the bush with burrs caught on his sleeve,
while, at the far end of an empty lot,
another child wanders where he's not been before.
I wonder what today will be
in ten years' time unless something is done
to uncover the bridge between the two extremes.
The hill stands, bearing witness over the shared soil
where seeds have sprouted swaying in the breeze.

GOING HOME AFTER WASHING
WINDSCREENS AT A CORNER STREET

In breaks of traffic lights the city bares
the latest round of politics and piling debt.
Seven o'clock. On the street the hot day lifts
its fears into the half-dark of the evening's quiet
malady. Behind a young boy going home,
the moon, like a snapshot in repose,
deepens its gaze to a place thoughts never roam;
(some man bereft of shame steps from a lamppost
ineptly glancing sideways, zipping up).

Soon he must cross to the lane where nothing's changed,
tiptoeing past the borderline and the day's hard luck,
passing the spot near the zinc gate where his brethren
fell into that bloody count. The moon retreats
behind the lignum vitae tree, and he
to his room, facing the flaking wooden wall
with a haloed Jesus Christ astride a donkey
in His calm wisdom, treading the green palm leaves
which coated the graveled road to Palm Sunday.

In a church next door, near the corner shop, palms rise
invoking the Holy Ghost. A human voice lifts a prayer
for the mother unable to rise from the day
of her son's affliction at the boot of authority,
when the leaves of the ginger lily shook in the wind
like devastation under a September sky.

Dawn creeps over the lane with a fresh intonation.
Nothing significant comes because of it.
Still, he puts on the rollerblades of wishful thinking
where bougainvillea spills over the fence, and dreams
past the ripped shirt-tails in the barbed wire's fist,
over the prickled fence of his father's chosen country

to a place where he can fall in love and feel
his young life poised to fashion something with wings.

WATCHING THE WAR

Watching the war, and wondering what's to come
to pass in the next few months and years –
what is so utterly invisible as tomorrow?

Not love,
not the wind,
not the growing shadow
of a fast descending hawk,
nor the grief sprouting
from the foliage of its first phase.
Not the river meandering
from last week's stream
down tracks that end in the sea.
Nothing.

And yet how often I try to look ahead!
But I hear only the blow-by-blow
talk, and the jostling in the desert
where the burden of history
rises, like dust roiled by the wind,
at loose ends, hitting the sky
with death two steps away.

I see a father who cannot protect his child
from the echo of the horror,
a mother on the verge of longing,
as if wishing to live her life backwards
to where the hen gathered her chickens
under her wings; dreading tomorrow,
knowing that this day will shake her awake
years from now on a December night.

I do not know where uncertainty comes from,
but I see a time for loss

to build its tower in the yard,
for the minds running on instinct
to be troubled by the moon;
I see a silence etched by a burning candle
next to the one who will bring
the fresh rose to the tombs – speechless
over the just ploughed ground,
wondering for the soul's sake
what will be born, even out of a mistake.

CHRISTMAS MORNING BLUES

It's Christmas morning and through her blank stare
she's lost track of time, coming to terms with the ache.
It's not a day to sit with friends over talk,
or to count calories, but a day to go alone
to the bedrock of the 60s, where history rises
in a room overlooking Kingston Harbour's
darkened murmur as it slaps against the wall
where once she fluttered up a fee-fee racket,
and threw fire clappers at a shivering dog.

A day to go back to the crux of the past
where the grandmarket morning shapes
a father carrying a child on his shoulder,
who, out of fear, closes one eye
as she still watches the masquerade
drumming down the street,
to what she still carries wherever she goes
in a world where disbelief wraps its blanket
around her as she tiptoes along the edge
of her own dead child vanishing.

Still hoping for some blessing in disguise,
she wakes in the bed of a thousand questions
emptying through their hourglass to a still life:
to a well-known voice coming back through the leaves,
and through the ghost of a wind barely stirring
the blood-red poinsettia shivering outside her door.

The sun slashes through the cracks
of the shut wooden louvres as though daring the dark
she's working hard to corner
for a glimpse of what's going on inside:
that which she cannot put into words.

TO JAMAICA, AT THE BREAK OF DAY

"Perhaps in this neglected spot is laid
Some heart once pregnant with celestial fire;
Hands, that the rod of empire might have sway'd,
Or waked to ecstasy the living lyre."
(Thomas Gray: 'Elegy Written in a Country Churchyard')

A siren wails in the approaching dawn.
A harsh wind infuses the leaves with what it knows.
A jellyman pitches his handcart stall and waits.
Madness ticks on the heels of June.

It's said that every defeated gesture implies
the past. Under this fogged-in city hillside
a lame result mocks the young now forced
to grow like victims on yesterday's tears.

No map on which to draw the dead-end road,
to sketch the terror in black and white,
the choice leading to the wrong thing still!

They're forced to watch, as if chained to a train,
the wheels of power dally round the cause
(as if written in stone) of casting blame,
the dry blood of a nation at the feet
of a five-year, term-after-term, elusive, plan.

I write this poem to record
that a past which fails the future is a wall
cleared of old faces, old photographs,
from which memory bounces like a rubber ball,

that, beneath this leftover moon,
witness to midnight blues since time began,
a fledgling of hope awaits the sun.

CHRISTMAS EVE

Christmas eve some years ago, alone
(the office closed half-day)
I held my own, easing into the fact
of being half-way
between a childless divorce, and no affair —
drifting like a leaf in the stream of city traffic
under a noonday sun with nothing to prepare,
no cake to bake. My mind connects
a classic childhood memory dancing into view
among the fee-fee racket: passing two dogs
doing it, and some man who's had a few
too many. I return to the Christmas tree's
blinking to the drummer boy's *pa-rap-a-pom-pom*
and suddenly hunger for wine, for the beat of a drum.

FROM A COVE IN ST. ANN

From under the noonday shadow of a rock
I stare long and hard into the blue
sea, breaking one thought to ponder through
to the heart of a concern, taking stock
of a home where shocking news is the norm.
It's hard to put a finger on the lessons
to be learned; as when a tense bow misses
a shifting target, each moment ends in doubt.
On a day like this, besieged between 'forlorn'
and a place riddled with brutalities, I
distract myself with the waves rushing to shore,
and the blessings one must create to know the sea's.
I lift my hope over the open water
with its flush of foam which alters in the sand,
filtering its sound to the hill as if to find
an echo far from the turbulent deep. Dusk
drops over the trees where some unknown soul
stumbled once, with one hand breaking his fall.

LOOKING AROUND

Putting my best foot forward, tiptoeing through a town
reeking with the hot jerk-chicken smell of fear,
a town over which the hills stand still,
I browse through a room with paintings on its walls
as through a temporary shelter from a storm.

The first that arrests me, '*The Child Of The City*',
takes me to a place that requires no light:
waxed into public view, a young boy stares
from beyond a barbed-wire fence. His gaze
is difficult to engage, plunged to another place
with a look one keeps for when no one's around.

It isn't hard to imagine some voiceless world
in which his future's fixed, somewhere in the past,
like words locked in a pen in which the ink goes dry.
With his shoulders to the wall, beneath an unlit sky
too shadowed to make out, rich-brown and deep-red
upward strokes make darkness visible; and he
is a question mark in a khaki shirt, unbuttoned
all the way up, palms crossed, hand over empty hand.

IN A CROWN OF THORNS

Like moving towards a corner, He saw his death
coming, carrying the Cross to the hour of gloom,
heart-torn between two worlds and out of breath
He was crowned with the thorn known for its winter bloom,
and mocked by a surge of dissatisfied men
itching for a miracle, like the one
at Galilee when He walked on water, or
turned stones to bread when His work had just begun.
But the greatest was to see how a brave man died
bleeding without a word that whoever wished might rise
in sweet soul-surrender heavenward,
enduring the driven nails
till the sun sank, taking His shadow back
into the womb of Time, the higher rock.

9/11

When the gift of laughter hardens to stone
there's nothing much that one can do with words.
When the latest call becomes the last call home
and the atmosphere is wreathed in disbelief,
the heart knits into knots.
A voice is singing along the Hudson river
stretching into the night for the child who left
her raggedy-ann doll behind before she was done
with it; fished from the rubble with smoke in its eyes
under an ashen sky. The river runs
where the moon still treads the darkened water
as if in search of a vacant spot
in which to pour the grieving.
Like a candle drifting in a paper boat,
this is a fragile world.
The rules of the game are changing.
The sky is silent over where the World Trade Center stood.

CHANCES ARE

Coming in from the streets that mock delight
I'm caught between two streams of thought:
old news, and the need to shift my mind to write.
A melting candle moves tobacco from the flat,
and, short of throwing both hands up in the air,
solutioned-out in a world where all's been said.
I plan never to compare today
but do what I have to, pushing ahead,
fishing around these potential days
in a land spinning on the edge of nerves
where someone's always leaving, and someone else is busy.
Rights are taken further away from those they serve.
Chances are the prime minister will not come to see
me or my friends. He's busy. So are we.

ON NEW YEAR'S EVE

Lighting each candle with another,
sipping Calvados, counting down the hour
to the midnight bells in this hard country,
I walk west while the years unzip themselves
turning my back on the uneasy dawn
on the last day of the year.

Away from the dawn of another war
with its swarm of uncertainties,
with everything poised along the same road,
pondering the words for what's guttering
out of the anger in the air.
I leap across my own synapses
to when I learnt to do the twist
and chatted about Chubby Checker
as though he lived next door,

Come on, baby, let's do the twist,
oooh-yeah, and it goes like this

rocking the hips, arms up and down
cutting the wind, taking a spin on my partner's arm,
dancing the dance as we did last summer,

to when I got caught in the rain with no place to go
but the dampening grass at the far end of a field
under the old poinciana with the woodpecker's hole,
the blood's wild tree which survived the storm
behind which ancestors might be sipping double white rums.
There was the branch at the forest's edge
which itched like hell, and the egrets glided
over the hill where the fish in their pond
swam, while the bamboo leaves soughed in the wind,
shaking off the last of the rainwater.

The morning fogged in, awaiting the sun
at that time of year when, almost every day,
my father trailed off to his garden of thought
where the yam vines leaned from overweight,
sinking into the hour as into a soft pillow –
where he took back half his soul.

I think that whatever returns, returns
to find its voice,
and that, if I walk far enough
I may find the words for that morning.

ABOUT THE AUTHOR

Delores Gauntlett was born in Jamaica in 1949. She studied Accounting and Business Administration and has worked for many years in the manufacturing sector. Her poems have appeared in *The Caribbean Writer*, London Poetry Society's *Poetry News*, *Kunapipi*, *Hampden-Sydney Review*, *The Observer's Literary Arts*, *German-Bayswater Textbook* and others. Her first collection, *Freeing Her Hands to Clap*, while a manuscript-in-progress, won a highly commended award in the 1999 National Book Development Council biennial competition (Jamaica).

OTHER JAMAICAN POETRY TITLES FROM PEEPAL TREE

Opal Palmer Adisa, *Caribbean Passion*
1-900715-92-9 £7.99

Lloyd Brown, *Duppies*
0-948833-83-1, £6.95

Kwame Dawes, *Progeny of Air*
0-948833-68-8, £7.95

Kwame Dawes, *Prophets*
0-948833-85-8, £7.95

Kwame Dawes, *Jacko Jacobus*
0-948833-85-8, £7.95

Kwame Dawes, *Requiem*
0-948833-85-8, £5.99

Kwame Dawes, *Shook Foil*
1-900715-14-7, £7.99

Kwame Dawes, *New and Selected Poems*
1-900715-70-8, £9.99

Marcia Douglas, *Electricity Comes to Cocoa Bottom*
1-900715-28-7, £6.99

Gloria Escoffery, *Mother Jackson Murders the Moon*
1-900715-24-4, £6.99

John Figueroa, *The Chase*
0-948833-52-1 £8.95

Jean Goulbourne, *Woman Song*
1-900715-57-0, £6.99

Rachel Manley, *A Light Left On*
0-948833-55-6, £5.99

Earl McKenzie, *Against Linearity*
0-948833-85-8, £7.95

Earl McKenzie, *The Almond Leaf* (forthcoming)
1-84523-012-4, £7.99

Anthony McNeill, *Chinese Lanterns from the Blue Child*
1-900715-18-X, £6.99

Geoffrey Philp, *Florida Bound*
0-948833-82-3, £5.95

Geoffrey Philp, *Hurricane Center*
1-900715-23-6, £6.99

Geoffrey Philp, *Xango Music*
1-900715-46-5, £6.99

Velma Pollard, *Crown Point*
0-948833-24-6, £7.99

Velma Pollard, *Shame Trees Don't Grow Here*
0-948833-48-3, £6.99

Velma Pollard, *Leaving Traces* (forthcoming)
1-84523-021-3, £7.99

Heather Royes, *Days and Nights of the Blue Iguana*
1-84523-019-1, £7.99

Ralph Thompson, *The Denting of a Wave*
0-948833-62-9, £6.95

Ralph Thompson, *Moving On*
1-900715-17-1, £7.99

Ralph Thompson, *View from Mount Diablo*
1-900715-81-3, £7.99

Gwyneth Barber Wood, *The Garden of Forgetting*
1-84523-007-8, £7.99

All available from Peepal Tree Press's website, with secure, on-line ordering. Visit peepaltreepress.com
or contact us my mail at 17 King's Avenue, Leeds LS6 1QS, UK